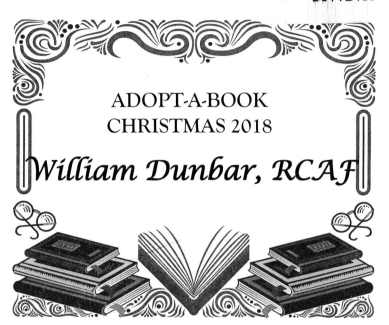

ADOPT-A-BOOK
CHRISTMAS 2018

William Dunbar, RCAF

VICTORY
1918
CELEBRATING THE
ARMISTICE
IN PHOTOGRAPHS

Cover illustrations © Mirrorpix

First published 2018

The History Press
The Mill, Brimscombe Port
Stroud, Gloucestershire, GL5 2QG
www.thehistorypress.co.uk

Images © Mirrorpix, 2018
Introduction © Peter Doyle, 2018

British Library Cataloguing in Publication Data.
A catalogue record for this book is available from the British
Library.

ISBN 978 0 7509 8565 9

Typesetting and origination by The History Press
Printed in Turkey by Imak

VICTORY
1918

CONTENTS

INTRODUCTION

'Aren't you excited? Hurrah! Hurrah! Hurrah! News reached here that peace is declared. Children excited. Thanksgiving service tonight. Whole day's holiday tomorrow!'

Postcard, 11 November 1918

The war officially ended with the Armistice of 11 November 1918, seemingly abruptly. However, in truth, the Central Powers had been crumbling during the autumn of 1918, with Germany's weaker allies feeling the pinch of shortages and the push of the Allied offensives. Bulgaria capitulated first, on 29 September; the Ottoman Empire followed on 30 October; Austria–Hungary on 3 November; and finally Germany herself on 11 November, at exactly 11 a.m. The news of the end of the war was received in many ways – for many British soldiers, its occurrence was almost matter-of-fact, a typical diary entry reading simply, 'Armistice signed with Germany': a few words to signify acceptance that all they had been through was now over. Popular newspapers such as the *Daily Mirror* made more of the occasion, and heralded a greater outpouring of public emotion.

The fall on the Western Front followed a succession of hammer blows that had been striking the German Army since the opening of the Battle of Amiens on 8 August 1918 – the beginning of 100 days of continuous Allied advance. During this advance, the Allied armies pushed the Germans back to a line that was broadly similar to the one at which it had first met the British 'Old Contemptibles' at Mons, four years before. The terms of the Armistice with Germany that followed required the cessation of hostilities, the evacuation of occupied territory, the surrender of large quantities of arms and equipment, the internment of the High Seas Fleet, and the occupation of German soil. It was a bitter blow. For the returning German armies that had held back the Allies on the Western Front for so long, the arduous march back to the Fatherland served only to emphasise the scale of the defeat. And as they marched back, the sights and sounds of the new republic confronted them, leading to scapegoating that would have repercussions in the post-war world, set to ignite a future conflict.

The British Empire suffered more than 900,000 dead and over 2 million wounded, while the German losses and injured amounted to more than twice these figures. In all, at least 10–15 per cent of those who joined up were killed. While the majority returned, many were scarred in some way by their participation in the world war. Some twenty years after the end of the conflict, estimates of the casualties in Britain recognised some 12,000 amputees, 10,000 blind or visually impaired and 11,000 hearing impaired; 31,000 men suffered from shell shock. There is no wonder that the effects of the Great War lived on for decades after the Armistice.

In early 1917, discharged soldiers and sailors were mobilising in another arena: the political one. Voting in the 'khaki election' of 14 December 1918 were not only servicemen still in uniform, but also women over 30, who had been granted a vote for the first time. In calling the election, David Lloyd George was determined to 'deliver the peace'. At a meeting on 25 November 1918, he made a pledge by which he would be forever judged: 'What is our task? To make Britain a fit country for heroes to live in ...' Ultimately, his campaign promises would turn out to be hollow. With so many men demobilised in the depths of the post-war slump that followed the gearing of a nation for 'total war', finding employment was a nightmare task.

In France and Flanders, the people returned to find their towns destroyed, their farms devastated. Picking a living amongst the ruins, farmers tried to clear their land and rebuild what was possible on the old front line. And soon, the British men and women of the Great War were drawn back to the battlefields: old soldiers to see the fields of their endeavours and to seek out comrades; women and children to mourn husbands and fathers who still lay in Flanders Fields, remembering their own. In France and Flanders alone, the Imperial War Graves Commission was charged with the protection of over half a million graves and more than 1,200 cemeteries. It was to these cemeteries, graves and memorials that visitors came in numbers during the early years of peace. In London, Lutyens' Centotaph, first built in wood before being made permanent in Portland stone, became the focal point for remembrance, while the Tomb of the Unknown Warrior, installed with great reverence in the entrance to Westminster Abbey, marked the nation's sacrifice.

The first British Poppy Day was held on 11 November 1921, the third anniversary of the end of the Great War. The origin of the remembrance poppy springs from the words of John McCrae's 1915 poem 'In Flanders Fields', but it was American Moïna Michael and Madame Guérin of France who first adopted the simple flower as a mark of remembrance during 1918–19. In 1921, poppies made their appearance in Britain, embraced by the British Legion. They were a success, the proceeds from their sale used then – and now – to support disabled and destitute servicemen and women.

This war had left a long shadow.

Peter Doyle
2018

THE END OF HOSTILITIES

11 November 1918: The signal from Allied headquarters to British forces on the Western Front, informing them of the start of the ceasefire and armistice on the 11th hour of the 11th day of the 11th month.

September 1918: A view of Menin Gate and the road that led to the front line in Ypres, Belgium.

26 September 1918: Soldiers unloading a supply tank on the Somme during the final 100 days campaign that resulted in the Armistice being signed in November.

18 October 1918: The Liverpool Irish (8th Battalion, King's Liverpool Regiment), accompanied by a young French boy carrying a rifle, march triumphantly into Lille, northern France, to liberate the town from nearly four years of occupation.

11 November 1918: The railway coach where the Armistice
was signed in France.

11 November 1918: The Allied representatives at the signing
of the Armistice in the forest of Compiègne. Ferdinand Foch
is second from right.

Above left and right:
22 November 1918: The scene on the bridge of HMS *Queen Elizabeth*, the flagship of the Home Fleet, the day the German High Seas Fleet surrendered. Admiral David Beatty, Commander-in-Chief of the Home Fleet, is in the centre with the binoculars.

Right:
24 November 1918: German submarines of the High Seas Fleet shortly after they surrendered.

Although discussions opened in December 1918, the Peace Conference did not formally open until 18 January 1919. The Versailles Conference left two major legacies. Firstly, the harshness of the terms that Germany was forced to accept, in particular the scale of reparations she had to pay to her enemies, crippled her financially and led to German resentment and, indirectly, the rise of the Nazi Party. However, on a more positive note, the second legacy was the creation

28 November 1918: The German High Seas Fleet anchored in Scapa Flow after surrendering to the Allies at the end of the First World War.

of the League of Nations, a supranational organisation dedicated to the maintenance of world peace through collective security. Although incredibly ineffectual, the League became the forerunner to the United Nations.

Despite their protests and the resignation of their Chancellor, Phillip Scheidemann, Germany finally signed the Treaty of Versailles on 28 June 1919, five years to the day after the death of Franz Ferdinand. The treaty was so harsh largely due to the demands of France. David Lloyd George, the British Prime Minister, realised that the terms were far too hard on Germany and famously commented, 'We shall have to fight another war all over again in 25 years at three times the cost.'

He was, of course, wrong. The world only had to wait twenty years, not twenty-five.

1 January 1918: Left to right: David Lloyd George (standing, facing camera with walking stick), General Sir Henry Wilson and Marshal Ferdinand Foch (with cane under arm) en route for the Supreme War Council.

December 1918:
Representatives of the Allies
drafting the terms of the
Versailles Treaty.

13 January 1920: French
Premier Georges Clémenceau
seen here ratifying the
Treaty of Versailles for the
French Government.

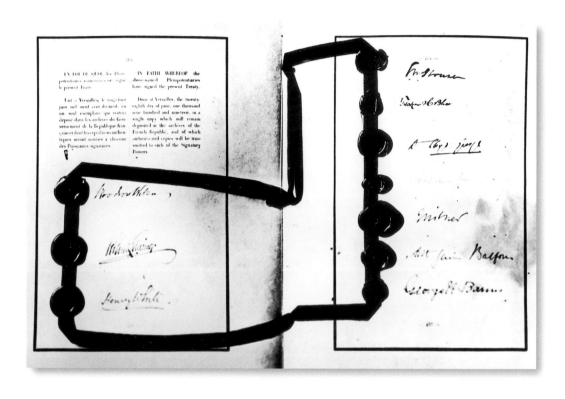

28 June 1919: British and American signatures on the Treaty of Versailles.

28 June 1919: British Prime Minister Lloyd George and French President Clémenceau arriving at a Peace Treaty party in Versailles.

28 June 1919: Signing of the Peace Treaty in the Hall of Mirrors at Versailles.

28 June 1919: Woodrow Wilson, the American President, leaving the Peace Conference.

28 June 1919: Crowds in the grounds of the Palace of Versailles shortly after the signing of the Peace Treaty.

28 June 1919: Woodrow Wilson (second from right) and General Pershing (third from right) at an Anglo-American banquet at the Palace of Versailles.

28 June 1919: Cheering crowds greet French Premier Georges Clémenceau (third from left), American President Woodrow Wilson (fifth from left in the top hat) and British Prime Minister David Lloyd George as they leave Versailles.

29 June 1919: Prime Minister Lloyd George with King George V leaving Victoria station by the Wilton Road approach. The King met his Prime Minister at the station platform on Mr Lloyd George's return from France, where he had signed the Peace Treaty at Versailles.

29 June 1919: Prime Minister David Lloyd George bidding farewell to France after signing the Peace Treaty.

29 June 1919: Prime Minister David Lloyd George, driving in an open horse-drawn carriage outside Buckingham Palace, on arrival from France after signing the Peace Treaty.

11 November 1918: German soldiers march back into Germany after crossing the Rhine at Cologne following the First World War Armistice.

1 December 1918: The first Christmas leave train departing northern Italy. The troops are happy, even if the mode of transport is somewhat crude.

1 January 1919: Coming Home. Men of the 8th Battalion, Manchester Regiment, marching along London Road, Manchester, on their return from Belgium.

29 January 1919: Women packing civilian suits. After being discharged from the army, every soldier was given the choice of a civilian suit or the sum of £2 12*s* 6*d*. A large proportion of them chose the suit, which was quickly supplied from the Royal Army Clothing Factory.

24 September 1919: The last of the women conductors taking a fare on a London bus. By 3 October 1919, all women conductors had been retired and replaced by men just returned from the First World War.

CELEBRATION

12 November 1918:
Daily Mirror front page:
'How London Hailed the
End of War'.

ALLIES' DRASTIC ARMISTICE TERMS TO HUNS

The Daily Mirror

CERTIFIED CIRCULATION LARGER THAN THAT OF ANY OTHER DAILY PICTURE PAPER

No. 4,696. TUESDAY, NOVEMBER 12, 1918 One Penny.

HOW LONDON HAILED THE END OF WAR

The King and Queen appeared on the balcony at Buckingham Palace to acknowledge the cheers of the crowd that gathered to congratulate their Majesties on the occasion.

How news of the armistice signature came over the wire to the newspaper offices. A facsimile of it as automatically printed on the tape machine. The cheers which greeted it were the first to be raised.

There never again will be such news for the Mercuries of the streets to cry. (*Daily Mirror.*)

A historic message as it came over the wire. It is dramatic that the last British war communiqué should proclaim our forces at Mons.

Goddesses in the car, accompanied by a man of war, celebrate the occasion. (*Daily Mirror.*)

Nothing gave greater satisfaction to all of us than the news that the cessation of hostilities found the British armies once more in possession of Mons...

11 November 1918: This mixture of soldiers and civilians took over a London taxi-cab for a joyride in Trafalgar Square.

11 November 1918: Crowds amassed outside Buckingham Palace, London.

Officers on horseback.

London Victory Parade at Hyde Park Corner.

Tanks and soldiers on parade.

Passing over Westminster Bridge with the Houses of Parliament in the background.

Above and opposite: Sailors at the London Victory Parade.

Massed colours of the British Army.

Field Marshal Sir Douglas Haig in the procession.

Marshal Foch in the procession.

Admiral Beatty in the procession.

Nurses in the procession.

The procession leaving Albert Gate.

General Pershing, who led the American Expeditionary Force,
in the procession.

The Women's Royal Naval Service on parade.

25 April 1919: The Prince of Wales and Field Marshal Haig seen here taking the salute on the steps of Australia House, London, during the Anzac Day march.

25 April 1919: Prince Edward, later King Edward VII, takes the salute as the Anzac troops march through London.

26 April 1919: Queen Alexandra stands outside the gates of Buckingham Palace to receive the salute from a march-past of troops.

4 May 1919: Victory Parade of Dominion troops march through London in celebration of their successful contribution to the Allied forces' efforts in the First World War.

4 May 1919: A spectator rushing to give a Canadian soldier a rose in Victoria Street, London.

May 1919: Canadian soldiers cleaning their uniforms in Hyde Park a few days before the Dominion troops are due to parade through London.

1 July 1919: General John J. Pershing, in London for the peace celebrations, leaving Victoria station with Winston Churchill.

King George V and Queen Mary seen here in Hyde Park watching the peace celebrations.

Dancing in Hyde Park.

The victory march passing down the Mall.

Members of the Royal Artillery parading through the streets of London.

Colonial and overseas troops marching up Whitehall in double column.

Field Marshal Sir Douglas Haig on horseback leads officers and soldiers through the crowded streets.

British and Allied troops marching through Trafalgar Square.

British and Allied troops pass Buckingham Palace.

Marshal Ferdinand Foch, Supreme Commander of the
Allied Armies in 1918, in the Peace Day procession.

Field Marshal Sir Douglas Haig.

Huge crowds gathering in Trafalgar Square.

The London Victory March passing Admiralty Arch; picture taken from a balloon.

The Thames Peace Pageant celebrated the efforts of British mariners and merchant seamen in the First World War. It was held in London on 4 August 1919, the fifth anniversary of Britain's declaration of war on Germany.

The start barge carrying the Royal Family.

Crowds gathered on the embankment and Westminster Bridge to watch the spectacle.

British and Allied troops marching through Trafalgar Square.

The small boats of the pageant following the royal barge along the Thames.

11 November 1918: Cambridge 'let itself go' with full vigour on receipt of the news that the Germans had accepted and signed the drastic Armistice terms of the Allies, and the rejoicing was kept up every evening throughout the week. An effigy of the Kaiser was hoisted on the point of a bayonet and carried through the streets, to be consigned to the flames of a Market Hill bonfire one evening. A cadet, attired as a padre, attended to the 'obsequies'.

Later processions of cadets met on the Market Hill engaged in a Big Push.
Premises occupied by the *Cambridge Magazine* at the corner of St John's Street
were wrecked by a crowd. Two other shops in the same occupation were treated
in similar fashion.

11 November 1918: Party time in Elswick, Newcastle, as residents of Tyneside Terrace celebrate.

Above and opposite:
11 November 1918: Victory Parade at George Square, Glasgow, in front of Lord Provost Welsh and service chiefs.

19 July 1919: The Great Victory Parade through Newcastle.

July 1919: Flags of the Allies adorn buildings in Grainger Street, Newcastle.

19 July 1919: A peace tea party held in Liverpool.

19 July 1919: A procession taking place during the Victory Parade at the Arc de Triomphe, Paris.

14 July 1919: Marshals Ferdinand Foch and Joseph Joffre at the Hôtel de Ville during the peace celebrations in Paris.

14 July 1919: Marshal Foch decorates a French soldier.

14 July 1919: Marshals Foch (left) and Joffre leading the victory parade in Paris.

THE FALLEN

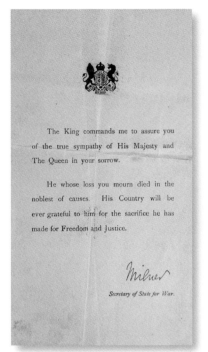

The King commands me to assure you of the true sympathy of His Majesty and The Queen in your sorrow.

He whose loss you mourn died in the noblest of causes. His Country will be ever grateful to him for the sacrifice he has made for Freedom and Justice.

Milner

Secretary of State for War.

No. _____

(If replying, please quote above No.)

ARMY FORM B. 104—82.

Infantry Record Office,

Warwick

11. 9. 1918.

Madam.

It is my painful duty to inform you that a report has been received from the War Office notifying the death of :—

(No.) 34886 (Rank) Private

(Name) Wilfrid Nicholson

(Regiment) 15th **ROYAL WARWICKSHIRE REGT.**

which occurred with the British Expeditionary Force on the 30th August 1918

The report is to the effect that he was killed in action

By His Majesty's command I am to forward the enclosed message of sympathy from Their Gracious Majesties the King and Queen. I am at the same time to express the regret of the Army Council at the soldier's death in his Country's service.

I am to add that any information that may be received as to the soldier's burial will be communicated to you in due course. A separate leaflet dealing more fully with this subject is enclosed.

I am,

Madam.

Your obedient Servant, Lieut. Colonel,

c/o Infantry Records

No. 7 DISTRICT

Officer in charge of Records.

8820. Wt. W6452/P549. 150M. 1/18. T. & W Ld. Forms B 104—82T.

P.T.O.

11 September 1918: Letters from the front informing Wilfrid Nicholson's mother of his death and a sympathy note from the King and Queen.

As it so happens, these letters were a mistake and Nicholson was alive, saved by his cigarette tin, but not every mother was so lucky.

Late 1918: Soldiers collecting plants and flowers in their spare time to decorate the graves of their fallen comrades.

10 November 1918: A Canadian artillery man tries to amuse a little Belgian baby. The mother was killed and the child, who was in her arms, was wounded by a German shell.

14 February 1919: General Currie visits the graves of 200 civilians who were shot against a wall on 21 August 1914 in Andenne.

11 November 1919: The devastated city of Ypres seen from the air a year after the war had ended. In the centre of the picture are the remains of the Cloth Hall and the Cathedral.

11 November 1920: The Funeral of the Unknown Soldier in Paris; the procession is about to enter boulevard Saint-Germain. Remains of the Unknown Soldier were then carried to the Arc de Triomphe in a solemn procession, where the coffin was placed in the chapel on the first floor.

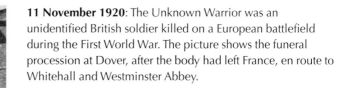

11 November 1920: The Unknown Warrior was an unidentified British soldier killed on a European battlefield during the First World War. The picture shows the funeral procession at Dover, after the body had left France, en route to Whitehall and Westminster Abbey.

11 November 1920: The railway van that conveyed the body of the Unknown Warrior from Dover to Victoria.

1 July 1980: Veterans of the First World War salute the memory of their comrades killed at the Battle of the Somme.

Behind three names on South Bank's war memorial lies the story of brothers-in-arms who paid the ultimate price during the First World War. Like many other young men, the Mates brothers – William, Henry and James – bravely went off to war, but none came home.

16 April 2015: Over100 years after they were killed in action in October 1914, six British soldiers are re-interred in the Commonwealth War Graves Commission Prowse Point Military Cemetery, near Ypres.

It was not possible to identify any of those being re-interred, although two served with the King's Own Regiment (Lancaster) and two with the Lancashire Fusiliers. The others are unknown.

COMMEMORATION

5 July 1919: A memorial to the eighteen children of the Upper North Street School who were killed during a daylight air raid on the capital by a German Gotha bomber on 13 June 1917.

11 November 1919: Soldiers both active and de-mobbed march past the Cenotaph in Whitehall on the first anniversary of Armistice Day.

11 November 1919: Workers of a munitions factory in Sheffield observe a minute's silence on Armistice Day in remembrance of the many soldiers who died in the First World War.

17 March 1920: Queen Alexandra unveils the memorial to nurse Edith Cavell, who was shot for treason by the Germans.

12 July 1924: Lord Derby unveils the Cenotaph in Manchester in St Peter's Square to honour the city's war dead. The memorial, flanked by twin obelisks, was designed by renowned British architect Sir Edwin Lutyens. Lord Derby was joined for the ceremony by Mrs Bingle, who had lost three sons in the war.

11 November 1925: Local people pay their respects at the Cenotaph in Manchester as they remember the soldiers who died.

1 June 1927: Construction workers and stonemasons pose under the arch of the nearly completed Menin Gate memorial to the 54,000 missing British and Commonwealth soldiers lost on the battlefields of the Ypres Salient. The memorial at Ypres is located at the eastern exit of the town and marks the starting point for one of the main roads that led Allied soldiers to the front line.

7 September 1929: Buglers playing the 'Last Post' at the Menin Gate war memorial in Ypres, Belgium.

11 November 1929: Inspector Langford and PC 150 Smith stand in the road to halt the traffic while the two minutes' silence takes place in Broadgate, Coventry.

3 November 1933: The British Legion Poppy Factory in Richmond, south-west London. It was founded in 1922 to offer employment opportunities to wounded soldiers returning from the First World War, creating remembrance products for the Royal Family and the Legion's annual Poppy Appeal.

11 November 1935: Albert Square, Manchester, during the two minutes' silence.

31662 PRIVATE
WILLIAM CULLEN
HIGHLAND LIGHT INFANTRY
27TH MARCH 1917 AGE 29

11 November 1939: Armistice Day in a French war cemetery.

11 November 2014: Military cadet, Harry Alexander Hayes, places the last ceramic poppy in the moat of the Tower of London to mark Armistice Day. The installation *Blood Swept Lands and Seas of Red*, by artists Paul Cummins and Tom Piper, consisted of 888,246 ceramic poppies – representing each of the Commonwealth servicemen and women killed in the First World War.

You may also enjoy …

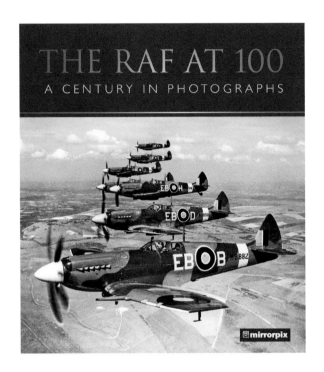

978 0 7509 8250 4